Gerard Manley Hopkins: the Lydiate Connections

and the Writing of 'Spring and Fall' in September 1880

Will Daunt
with illustrations by Susan Hodgkins
and an Afterword by Professor Joseph Feeney S.J.

Second Impression

Every effort has been made to check the copyright of materials used in this book.
Its text and photographs (except below*, or where untraceable) are © Will Daunt 2019 and 2020. Its drawings and cover painting are © Susan Hodgkins 2019, apart from the painting of Rose Hill in the body of the text, which is © Valerie Wright 1991.
*The photograph of Gerard Manley Hopkins is reproduced under licence from the National Portrait Gallery, and appropriate permissions to quote have been obtained from The Hopkins Quarterly, and Oxford University Press.
*The Afterword is © Professor Joseph Feeney S.J. 2019.

The drawing of Lydiate Hall on page 11 and the painting of St. Catherine's Chapel on page 14 belong to the National Trust - www.nationaltrust.org.uk. They are kept at Rufford Old Hall L40 1SG (about 15 kilometres from Lydiate), and are reproduced with kind permission.

Second impression is © Ormskirk Imprint 2020, ISBN 9780244165024

Any proceeds from the sale of *Gerard Manley Hopkins: the Lydiate Connections* will be donated to the charity Hospice Africa.

Hospice Africa is a Liverpool-based U.K. charity (no. 1024903) with a vision of "Palliative Care for all in need in Africa". For 25 years they have cared for and promoted care - including control of severest pain - for patients in Africa dying from cancer and other debilitating conditions. They have worked with governments, universities and initiators of palliative care units in 33 African countries, including Francophone countries. Now 35 of 54 African nations have palliative care, whereas in 1993 there were only three with any form of pain control or holistic care.
The charity provides funding for patient care and the training of health professionals at Hospice Africa Uganda (H.A.U.). Since 1993 H.A.U. has treated over 33,000 cancer patients in Uganda, trained over 10,000 nurses, doctors and medical students and prepared 873 community volunteers to help patients and their families. Millions more require this help in countries where cancer treatment reaches less than 10% in need.
"In palliative care we are on the coalface of death"
www.hospice-africa.org.uk

The Ormskirk Imprint is a small publishing enterprise based in West Lancashire. It works on a not-for-profit, commission-only basis, with any funds raised from book sales going to a nominated good cause.

Contents

Gerard Manley Hopkins comes to Lydiate	7
'Spring and Fall'	29
Afterword: An American Hopkins Scholar, A Jesuit, Visits Lydiate	39
Notes	43
Background Reading	46
Offshoots	47
A Hopkins Walk	49

Gerard Manley Hopkins comes to Lydiate

Hopkins in 1880

What is the greatest poem composed, or set, in South Lancashire? You might have your own favourite, but perhaps the *best known* was written by a lonely Jesuit priest, in the early autumn of 1880. This short guide is about the times, the people and the places which may shed some light on the writing of fifteen lines called 'Spring and Fall'.

Gerard Manley Hopkins' poetry - like that of Wilfred Owen - was almost unknown in his lifetime. Other writers encouraged him, and Robert Bridges ensured that his poems were first published properly in 1918, thirty or so years after Hopkins' death. Familiar works include 'The Windhover', 'Pied Beauty', 'God's Grandeur' and the much longer 'The Wreck of the Deutschland'. Including music and the visual arts, Hopkins' output is unlike that of any other English poet of the time. Often, he writes with the same energy and originality with which Van Gogh uses a paintbrush. Arguably, he is England's greatest Catholic poet of the modern age.

Brought up in London, Hopkins was the oldest son of committed Anglicans. His father was head of a firm that insured ships and their cargo against damage, as well as being a published poet and critic; his mother was a talented musician. The last of Hopkins' many siblings, Lionel, died in 1952, 63 years after his famous brother. But another brother, Felix, died in infancy.

In 1866, while studying at Oxford University, Hopkins was received into the Catholic Church by John Henry (later Cardinal) Newman - and he began his Jesuit training in 1868. His father and mother were unhappy about these decisions, and relations with them were difficult for a while. Later, this single-minded son became close once more to his parents and siblings. The many letters to his mother show how he was a considerate and loving son. In fact the religious life may well have strengthened the poet's relationship with his family. They were a constant as the Jesuits moved him to many different parts of Britain, and, finally, Dublin, where he died of typhoid fever in 1889, aged only 44.

Hopkins knew the older, enlarged county of Lancashire well, and before he arrived in Liverpool in January 1880, he had spent time in places like Stonyhurst College, and Leigh. Later, his ministry took him briefly to visit Preston, Maryport and Manchester. There was much that he liked about the county, no doubt including its distinctive Catholic heritage. He was fascinated by accents, and was a good mimic. But being moved from one parish to another made Hopkins' lifestyle unsettled.

The Jesuit church of St. Francis Xavier - or 'S.F.X.' as it's known locally - opened on Salisbury Street in central Liverpool in 1848. It can be seen above and is still there, and in early 1880 was serving a very large Parish. When Hopkins arrived, he became involved immediately in the life of the city and its Catholics, many of whom lived in poverty. He was part of a large team of priests, as the census for 1881 shows. Hopkins is the seventh name down:

Hopkins found life in Liverpool hard, perhaps because of his poor health and artistic temperament. Here was a young

10

priest who was expected to minister to parishioners of all ages, from birth to death, and the squalor that he saw tarnished his opinion of the city. The pulpit at S.F.X., from which he preached, can be seen on page 12.

Hopkins' powerful poem 'Felix Randal', shows how the poet was committed to his parish duties. The sonnet celebrates the life of the 31 year old Felix Spencer. Hopkins ministered to him and Felix died of T.B. on 21 April 1880 in Birchfield Street. That road remains a short walk from S.F.X., although none of its original houses have survived.

FELIX RANDAL

Felix Randal the farrier, O is he dead then? my duty all ended,
Who have watched his mould of man, big-boned and hardy-handsome
Pining, pining, till time when reason rambled in it, and some
Fatal four disorders, fleshed there, all contended?

Sickness broke him. Impatient, he cursed at first, but mended
Being anointed and all; though a heavenlier heart began some
Months earlier, since I had our sweet reprieve and ransom
Tendered to him. Ah well, God rest him all road ever he offended!

This seeing the sick endears them to us, us too it endears.
My tongue had taught thee comfort, touch had quenched thy tears,
Thy tears that touched my heart, child, Felix, poor Felix Randal;

How far from then forethought of, all thy more boisterous years,
When thou at the random grim forge, powerful amidst peers,
Didst fettle for the great grey drayhorse his bright and battering sandal!

A "farrier" is a specialized kind of blacksmith, and the poem celebrates Felix's strength and skill, just as it regrets his final illness. Furthermore, the second quatrain describes the spiritual support that Hopkins gave to Felix, which

might have been the right place for a priest to end a poem like this one. But the sestet that follows - written for one man from another - shows no religious theme. Interestingly, and as a younger man, Hopkins had thought his writing and his mission as a Jesuit to be incompatible, and he gave up poetry for a time. You might wonder at the change to Felix's surname. More of that later ...

The Jesuits in Salisbury Street had a number of missions in and around the city. For centuries, they had provided priests for the Catholic families who lived at Lydiate Hall. The original building - constructed for the Ireland family - included a number of priest's holes.

Peacocks keep watch at The Hayloft

During the late nineteenth and early twentieth century, the Hall was neglected. What remains is about a kilometre north of Lydiate, on the A5147, but you will see first the farm shop and pleasant Hayloft tea rooms which occupy some outbuildings of what was once a Tudor mansion.

Lydiate Hall in 1834
Courtesy of the National Trust, Rufford Old Hall

There's a duck pond and this attractive corner of Lydiate is patrolled by many boisterous peacocks.

Stopping for refreshment, you will be able to include a short walk round the site and gain some idea of the impressive size and appealing aspects of the old house and its surrounding woodland. In early spring, snowdrops and daffodils are particularly striking, amongst the visible ruins.

St. Catherine's Chapel is on the same side of the road (but a hundred metres or so nearer the village). Just as atmospheric as the Hall, this is known locally as "The

The well at Lydiate Hall (Susan Hodgkins)

Abbey", and was built by the Ireland family between 1475 and 1480. But it's been ruined since the Reformation. Ironically, the remains have survived the centuries better than those of the Hall. Both have weather-beaten information boards, but no sign from the road.

St. Catherine's (Susan Hodgkins)

At the foot of its main staircase, the National Trust's Rufford Old Hall has a painting of St. Catherine's, from about 1825. By the minister at Kirkby, it's a sentimental depiction of the building, less ruined and with fewer trees than now. Notice the pond in the bottom right hand corner. This no longer exists.

St. Catherine's Chapel, Rev. Robert Cort (1762-1850)
Courtesy of the National Trust, Rufford Old Hall

The ten or so visible graves are from the nineteenth century, and it is likely that Hopkins met some of the families that are remembered here. They have old Lancashire surnames, like Horrocks, Pemberton, Carfoot and Haskayne, and the poet might have known Thomas and Alice Lovelady, whose two infant children were buried here in 1856 and 1863. A damaged grave probably belongs to one of the Lythgoes, a Catholic family who figure later in this book.

But Hopkins might have been more interested in the Jesuits' records. These show that at least three of their priests

Graves at St. Catherine's

had been buried within the walls of the chapel, in the early 18th century. The resting places of Fathers Waldegrave, Draper and Mostyn (or Mosson) are unmarked.

Next to the Chapel is The Scotch Piper, an impressive pub with a thatched roof, which was built in the fourteenth century. It serves excellent beer.

The Jesuit connection can be seen at Our Lady's Church, too. This can be found along Hall Lane, on the other side of Southport Road from the tea rooms. It's most likely to be open before and after Mass. In Hopkins' time there was even a small spire, but this was removed for safety reasons in the first half of the twentieth century.

Many Jesuit priests are buried within its churchyard.

At the back of Our Lady's are sections of a remarkable alabaster reredos - or altar piece - rescued from St. Catherine's

Chapel. They depict the life and death of its patron saint in intricate detail.

Part of St. Catherine's Reredos (now at Our Lady's)

Inside the church, a centenary stained glass window commemorates the nearby chapel:

If you walk away from the tower and its north door, you'll notice the distinctive marble grave on your right, facing away from the path.

This was built for the Lightbound family, who lived at Rose Hill House on Pygons Hill Lane, which is about 1500 metres away. Thomas Lightbound had converted to Catholicism and was one of several Catholics who organized the foundation of St. Francis Xavier's church, back in Liverpool. Lightbound's brother-in-law Randal was a senior English Jesuit and was one of the priests who served Lydiate Hall.

As well as saying Mass at the Hall, the Jesuits played their part in supporting the newly built church of Our Lady's, providing priests for a few years after its 1854 opening. They also sent priests - including Gerard Manley Hopkins - to say

Mass for villagers and the Lightbounds at the family home in Lydiate.

Thomas is buried at Our Lady's, along with his wife Catherine and a number of his many children. While Catherine (who was a Lythgoe) had died about five years before Hopkins' arrival in the village, some of Thomas's adult offspring would have known the poet when he was still ministering from Liverpool. The 1881 census records that Charles and Gertrude Mary Lightbound were living with their widowed father, who was about 70. A second Gertrude Mary (Withnell) - Thomas's granddaughter - was also staying.

The Hall, the Abbey, the pub, the church? Hopkins would not have *needed* to visit any of these places but (with the probable exception of the pub ...) he might well have *wanted* to see them all. His base, Rose Hill House, was about twenty minutes walk away, and we know that he liked exploring. The guided walks at the end of this book give some impression of the places that he might have discovered.

Thomas had two sons living in Aughton. In 1881, Randal lived at Moss Side, Prescot Road and John at 162 Town Green. Having married two sisters (Mary and Annie Bradley), the brothers worked in Liverpool for a venerable cotton broker called Musgrove. By chance, and when travelling by train from Rose Hill early in 1880, Hopkins met Mr. Musgrove. The meeting went badly, with Hopkins' more right-wing views upsetting this Liberal pillar of the community.

As Hopkins put it:

> I talked so outrageously against Liberals and worse that Mr. Musgrove was shocked and hurt.

We can imagine how appalled the Lightbound brothers were by their chaplain's lack of tact, and, after one failed opportunity for peace-making, Randal Lightbound ensured that honour was restored between merchant and Jesuit. In his description, Hopkins is amusing about himself - but also fairly scornful of Randal's younger brother, who the poet thought to be too much of a slave to his employer:

> Luckily I was with the more genial Randal Lightbound, not with Mr. Musgrove's highpriest John. It took place on a bitter cold morning by a glowing waiting-room fire by Town Green Station. I advanced and ate humble pie ravenously, Mr. M was very good natured and himself finished the dish.

Although it took a couple of months to arrange Hopkins' apology, he went on to include Randal's name in the poem about the farrier. You can imagine the scene with Musgrove if you walk through the entrance to Town Green Station today.

To your right is the waiting room where Hopkins made amends. Now, he would struggle to recognise its interior, since it has become its own mini-*police*-station, managed by Lancashire Constabulary.

There are no cells, and you are unlikely to gain entry. Apparently the area has been 'policified', with none of the original fittings visible.

Town Green Station (Susan Hodgkins)
The old waiting room was beneath the chimneys

Other rooms on the city-bound platform have been adapted and divided into a ticket office, staff room and cleaner's stores. But on the Ormskirk-bound platform, a smaller, unfurnished building gives a better idea of how the place might have felt in 1880, with its various chimneys and fireplaces.

We don't know how Hopkins got from the railway to Rose Hill. The house was sold after Thomas Lightbound's death in 1895, and the sale records show that the family kept a "Capital Brougham" and a "Parisian Phaeton", which might have been sent to collect him.

Normally, the poet probably used Maghull station, rather than Town Green, because it's closer to the city. These days - as in the walk suggested later - you might choose to approach Lydiate from Maghull, via the Leeds and Liverpool Canal.

But the waterway was very busy in the early 1880s. With the introduction of some steam-powered traffic, this might have been just the kind of grimy thoroughfare Hopkins wanted to avoid: the equivalent of today's A59!

If walking from Maghull, it's more likely that he would

The Leeds and Liverpool Canal at Pilling Lane (Susan Hodgkins)

have taken the direct route through what was then only a village, down peaceful Damfield Lane and past St. Andrew's Church.

One thing's for sure: if he strayed west towards the site of Sefton and Maghull, or Lydiate Stations, the most that he might have seen would have been railway surveyors: the Southport and Cheshire Lines Extension didn't open until 1884.

Rose Hill House has always been a family home, and should be respected as such. It's set back discretely, on the inside of a bend in Pygons Hill Lane. From the road, you can see a large eighteenth-century country house, double-fronted and with the sweep of a generous drive. It's a listed building, with many sashed and bay windows. The facade was completed in the nineteenth century and the west wing probably added later. There are many trees which fill the garden and form a small wood on the south-west side of the property.

John Lightbound died young, and his oldest child, Ann Menken, writes of the house in its heyday:

Rose Hill House (Valerie Wright)

... that lovely old house with every luxury of those days, servants – carriages – a home farm and outdoor

> staff devoted to them, who had spent their lives with them and known my father and uncles from infancy ... It was a lovely place for the grandchildren and some of them were always there. They were certainly looked up to and respected "gentry" who thought of everyone around.

But elsewhere, Ann describes how two of her maiden aunts "fell upon hard years", after Thomas' Lightbound's death, and the sale of Rose Hill. "Cathy" and the aforementioned "Gerty":

> lived at 13 Salisbury Street (now pulled down) and which had been Uncle Frank's house ... They lived in a flat. I think the S.J.s has [sic] that house from Uncle Frank and in hard times they offered it to these two – rentless I think – out of gratitude to the Lightbound family ... Every morning for years these two maiden aunts crossed to SFX's Sacristy and kept it in order ...

Catherine and Gertrude - who, as young women would have known Hopkins - outlived him by forty-two and fifty years respectively.

It's not difficult to imagine the poet arriving at Rose Hill, and enjoying the escape from the city and his parish work, as he stepped into such a peaceful and protected world. He writes that:

> Every week, one of our community goes to Lydiate,

to a Catholic country house, to say mass next morning and return.

In a later letter, Hopkins tells his friend Robert Bridges that he is "often here for the night", although he mistakenly calls the house "Rose Hall".

The Lightbounds kept an upstairs room as an Oratory, where Hopkins or his fellow Jesuits would say Mass for the family and neighbours. The gaps in this section of Ann's notes are sadly illegible:

> There was the chapel in the house + that good privilege of reserving the Blessed Sacrament - a very perfect Chapel with windows which [...] morning Mass [...] shadows of all colours from the stained glass windows and a [...] Sacristy with vestments fitted chests etc.

But when the house was sold, its inventory gave no indication of a room devoted to worship: by then, the family might have been using the nearby church of Our Lady.

And the Lightbound presence in the church is formidable. Randal commissioned the enormous altarpiece to Our Lady's. It affirms the Lightbounds' influence on the Catholic and wider community in Lydiate.

The Lightbound Altar at Our Lady's: the top inscription names Randal and his wife Mary, while the central one is dedicated to Randal's father Thomas. At the base, Thomas's wife Catherine is remembered

It also obscures completely the east window, which visitors like Hopkins would have seen properly at the time of his stay in the area.

'Spring And Fall'

Although Hopkins' health was frail, he liked being outdoors. His letters tell of trips that he took from S.F.X. In January 1881, there was one towards Gill Moss (where the Jesuits sustained a Mission until 1887). Hopkins was rescued by two children from the "deep drifts frozen hard as night". The present day Gill Moss - with its various developments - would be unrecognisable to the poet.

He also recalls a walk by the frozen River Mersey in the same month:

> Well, I went. The river was coated with dirty yellow ice from shore to shore; where the edges could be seen it seemed very thick; it was not smooth but many broken pieces framed or pasted together again; it ... was floating down stream with the ebb tide; it everywhere covered the water, but was not of a piece, being continually broken, ploughed up, by the plying of the steam ferryboats, which I believe sometimes cannot make their way across.

But it was a stroll on 7 September 1880 that set his imagination wandering in a different direction. He describes it as something written while "walking from Lydiate". In a letter that he sent just after the first draft had been finished, Hopkins seems almost to dismiss his most recent writing:

> I enclose a little piece composed since I began this letter, not founded on any real incident. I am not

well satisfied with it ...

He's describing 'Spring and Fall', a remarkable fifteen- line poem which is different from anything else he produced:

SPRING AND FALL

to a Young Child

MÁRGARÉT, áre you gríeving
Over Goldengrove unleaving?
Leáves, líke the things of man, you
With your fresh thoughts care for, can you?
Áh! ás the heart grows older
It will come to such sights colder
By and by, nor spare a sigh
Though worlds of wanwood leafmeal lie;
And yet you wíll weep and know why.
Now no matter, child, the name:
Sórrow's spríngs áre the same.
Nor mouth had, no nor mind, expressed
What heart heard of, ghost guessed:
It ís the blight man was born for,
It is Margaret you mourn for.

The poem's subtitle is 'to a Young Child' and it addresses that girl, 'Margaret' as a letter might. There is no comfort for her sorrow at the coming of autumn, and the "wanwood leafmeal" everywhere. Hopkins was working on the poem as the Lancashire autumn - with its gently changing colours - took hold. The poem captures how feeling sad about the passing of time can be one of the burdens of growing up.

The accents on some letters indicate where Hopkins wanted the stresses to fall in each line, in the particular 'sprung' and falling rhythm which he invented.

'Margaret' is an English version of the Greek for 'pearl'. But who is *this* Margaret? Hopkins suggests that 'Spring and Fall' is an imagined situation. It's an unusual one too because it addresses a child, so directly. Also, this is a poem by a priest which - like the conclusion to 'Felix Randal' - has no Christian message.

There was no "Margaret" at Rose Hill House and no "Goldengrove" anywhere near Lydiate, so scholars have generally accepted that Hopkins invented these names, and imagined a girl called Margaret.

But did he?

Hopkins addressed poems like 'Felix Randal' to people that he knew. During his time in Liverpool, he found little inspiration, but he did write two other poems that are addressed to acquaintances. 'Brothers' is based on an incident which took place at "Mount St. Mary's in Derbyshire" and 'At The

Wedding March' recalls a Parish wedding at Bedford, Leigh. Two of these poems altered real people's names.

At Rose Hill, Hopkins must have met some of Thomas Lightbound's many grandchildren. However, his letters mention none of them, and this helps to explain why Margaret has remained a fiction in readers' minds.

Yet would it have been appropriate to name a real child? In September 1880, Hopkins was returning to his duties after a summer break, certainly in part with his extended family. These were often taken with his younger brother, Arthur, who was a popular Victorian painter and illustrator, working for *Punch* and *The London News*. Arthur's drawings accompanied the stories of Wilkie Collins and Thomas Hardy (notably in the latter's *The Return Of The Native*). Like his older brother,

Arthur Hopkins: Marine Study, Lyme Regis

he was fascinated by the challenge of painting the sea.

In 1880, Arthur's daughter Beatrice - who at that time was Hopkins' only niece - was about six years old. In 1946, a year or two before she died, Beatrice wrote down her memories of her Uncle Gerard.

She describes herself as "a small and a delicate one", something that Hopkins echoes in a letter to his mother of 1879. He enquires about Beatrice's "precocious rheumatism".

In turn, Beatrice remembers how her uncle used to "come, sit by my bed, and talk to me". She goes on to say that "his kindness and sympathy were un-failing" and describes how Hopkins would often holiday in London or Whitby with her family.

She also says:

> He was extraordinarily lucid – would explain things to me as a child. He went to the heart of it and cleared the air. It was all done so simply, yet everything became clear.

So, in September 1880, is it possible that Hopkins was remembering these "precocious" chats with Beatrice, as well as the fun he'd had on holiday? Returning to the challenge of Parish work in the inner city - where he had led a number of infant funerals - he might well have had mixed emotions when "walking from Lydiate". Thoughts of his lonely and challenging life as a priest, and the gulf between Liverpool and anyone from his family, might well have combined with the prospect of autumn. Of course, the trees of early September would have remained in leaf for a couple of months more, but it's the anticipation of their falling that seems to have set Hopkins' mood.

At the same time, surely the presence of the Lightbound children at Rose Hill would have reminded him of his own childhood, and his young niece.

Arthur's family often took holidays in Whitby with Gerard, and the brothers painted and drew together (a lesser artist, Gerard could be very critical of the long-suffering Arthur's work). About a mile inland from Whitby, there is a wood and a hamlet called Golden Grove.

To reach Golden Grove is - and was - easy. Whitby's East and West Cliffs slope down to the River Esk, which could be crossed in Hopkins' time by the predecessor to the current swing bridge. Walking along Church Street, on the river's east bank, they would have crossed Spital Bridge, passing shipyards run by John Turnbull, of the Whitby shipbuilding dynasty. He lived at Golden Grove.

The road then rises steeply to Larpool Lane.

Kelly's 1913 *Directory of the North and East Ridings of Yorkshire* describes the "charming glades" of Larpool Woods. Next to Larpool Hall, these were a "frequent resort of artists" and must have been known to the Hopkins brothers.

The River Esk from Larpool Viaduct

The Directory goes on to describe the path that leads "down the glen by the side of the pinetum and past Golden Grove".

These days you reach Golden Grove by walking under the bridge for the Scarborough railway - a line that did not open until 1885, and which closed in 1965.

Where Larpool Lane bends sharply to the right, you can continue straight ahead into Golden Grove's woodland. The stones along some sections of the footpath have clearly been there for a long time.

This is a charming and secluded place. The walk continues beside Cock Mill Beck and up to the hamlet of Golden Grove, passing its largely concealed waterfall.

So - if there is a Whitby connection to 'Spring and Fall' - why didn't Hopkins identify Beatrice, or tell her about the poem? It's easy to imagine that he might want to protect her - as much from the blunt message of the poem as from her identification by readers.

Of course, that's conjecture, but these suggestions followed numerous walks around Lydiate, somewhere that the poet grew to know during a period of loneliness and toil. Perhaps the poem was an attempt to exorcise some of his personal demons: his separation from his family; moments when he doubted his faith; the dread he felt at having to return to Liverpool.

And when you set foot in the hinterland of 'Spring and Fall' it's hard to believe that Hopkins' words are simply part of some imagined conversation, in a landscape that never existed.

The plaque outside Newman House in Dublin...

close to the room where Hopkins died on 8 June 1889

AFTERWORD: AN AMERICAN HOPKINS SCHOLAR, A JESUIT, VISITS LYDIATE
Joseph J. Feeney, S.J.
Saint Joseph's University, Philadelphia

It was a fine summer day in 1994 when two dear friends of mine from Widnes (once in Lancashire, now in Cheshire) drove me to visit the village of Lydiate, also in Lancashire. I was in England doing Hopkins research and I had gone to Widnes to spend a few days with my dear friends, the Billingsley family--Shelagh, Barry, and their sons Mark and Andrew. Dear friends that they are, they had often driven me to see places where Hopkins had worked: St. Francis Xavier's parish ("S.F.X.") in Liverpool, St. Joseph's Parish in Bedford Leigh near Manchester, Stonyhurst College in rural Lancashire, and St. Beuno's College in North Wales where both Hopkins and I had studied, he in 1874-77 and I in 1966-67. In North Wales, my friends and I also enjoyed many other sites which Hopkins might well have seen: Conwy Castle, Orme's Head as it ended its mountain-range, flocks of sheep in fields by the Irish Sea, and the Victorian pier at Llandudno.

But I must return to Hopkins and Lydiate. As Shelagh, Barry, and I arrived at Lydiate and drove around the village, we enjoyed looking at the houses and pubs and canals and crumbled remnants of old buildings. The village, we quickly realized, had a gentle charm and beauty.

But the climax of our visit to Lydiate--our Hopkins climax--was at Rose Hill House, an 18th-century home where Hopkins (and other Jesuits from Liverpool's "S.F.X.") celebrated Sunday Mass for the Lydiate Catholics who at that time had no resident priest. Before our trip I had contacted the family living in Rose Hill House, the Gilby family, and they said we'd be most welcome to visit and walk through their home and around their grounds, and see what Hopkins saw.

It was a beautiful summer day, and the Gilbys warmly welcomed us at the front door of Rose Hill House, showed us around the ground floor, then walked us up a flight of stairs to see the room where, they said, the visiting Jesuit had celebrated Sunday Mass. A large, round room, this "chapel" was painted white, and at the time of our visit had no furnishings--no chairs, no altar, no pictures. But it was beautiful in its stark simplicity and brightness, and while we were there, we spoke about the house's history and its importance for the whole village: how every Saturday a Jesuit from S.F.X. in Liverpool would take a train to Lydiate, sleep overnight, then celebrate Mass in the "chapel" at Rose Hill House. A warmth of relationship soon developed between priest and people, and decades later, we three visitors were at once moved, impressed, and grateful.

Then came a surprise for us--a touching example of the warmth and friendliness of the North of England and of the Gilby family: our hosts invited Shelagh, Barry, and myself to join them for lunch--a lunch prepared just for us and served at a table in the beautiful garden behind their house. I forget what we ate, but the food was delicious, the conversation lively, and the summer weather gently breezy. But I most remember--and still treasure--the hospitality and generosity of our lovely hosts at Rose Hill House, an example of Lydiate's warm and happy welcome to visitors.

It is perhaps fitting that Hopkins' most heartbreaking poem "Spring and Fall" was written in Lydiate, for it captures the human warmth and care so distinctive of Lydiate and England's North. As for Lydiate itself, Hopkins sent a copy of the poem to his friend and fellow poet Robert Bridges, adding "Lydiate, Lancashire, Sept. 7, 1880." Surely such a sensitive and heartfelt poem fits well the tone of Lydiate--a lovely gift of Hopkins from Lydiate to the world. Yes, "worlds of wanwood [may] leafmeal lie," but the poem "Spring and Fall" will never die, and will ever remain a remembrance and celebration of Lydiate and of life, a gift from their dear Fr. Hopkins, not only a fine priest but also a wondrous poet.

Rose Hill House in about 1900.
The note - probably by John Lightbound's daughter, Ann Menken - indicates that part of the first floor, where the "Priest's room, Chapel + Sacristy" could be found

Notes

The research behind this book involved a fair amount of reading, and my more technical account of its findings was published in the U.S.A. by The Hopkins Quarterly in the winter of 2018.

Much more important was the support provided by the people who guided the narrative in the right direction.

The late Gerard Swarbrick set me on the path(s) and Stephen Gilby of Rose Hill House provided invaluable time and information. Randal Lightbound's great grandson, Bernard Lightbound illuminated the family tree, and Sally Ralston and Bill from Merseyrail let me see behind the scenes at Town Green Station.

From "across the pond", Professor Joseph Feeney S.J. provided genial and generous encouragement while, back in Lydiate, David Witter literally and metaphorically opened for me the doors to Our Lady's Church.

Some curious things happened, along the way. When I first visited Rose Hill, Stephen showed me this piece of paper, which he had found, days before, hanging from a tree in the garden:

> 'And for all this, nature is never spent;
> There lives the dearest freshness deep down things;
> And though the last lights off the black West went
> Oh, morning, at the brown brink eastward, springs —
> Because the Holy Ghost over the bent
> World broods with warm breast
>   and with ah! bright wings.'
>
> Gerard Manley Hopkins
>   7 September 1880
>   Rose Hill

More intriguing is the mis-match between the date (when 'Spring and Fall' was first drafted), and the text, which is part of Hopkins' 'God's Grandeur'.

Later, as I turned out of Rose Hill's drive, I saw a kestrel floating above the road like the "windhover" in Hopkins' famous poem. I've never had a better sighting.

Margaret and Gerard are names recently heard around Rose Hill and, while Bill was showing me around the station, I explained my mission, and his eyes lit up. "S.F.X? That's my Parish Church".

Further symmetry can be found in the parallels between the vocations of Hopkins and the Founder of Hospice Africa, Professor Doctor Anne Merriman. Like Hopkins, she worked with the poor in the area around S.F.X. in Liverpool which was, as she says:

> still in a slum area when I practised geriatric medicine there in the '70s and the bull ring and other flats were still there housing mainly lonely old ladies and often their companionable fleas, hard to see in gas light....

And she recalls her time at University College Dublin where:

> for 5 years, I had lunch in Newman House and as a Nun with the Medical Missionaries of Mary said my prayers in the Church next door to the building [where Hopkins lived, worked and died].

The book's second impression followed a walk to Golden Grove, outside Whitby, about 140 years after the composition of 'Spring and Fall'.

W.D. Winter 2020

Background Reading

Most of these books are hard to track down. The various volumes of Hopkins' Collected Works are very pricey!

Bridges, R. (ed.) 2013 *Gerard Manley Hopkins Complete Poetical Works*. Hastings: Delphi Publishing

McDermott, J. (1997) *A Hopkins Chronology*. Basingstoke: Macmillan

McDermott, J. (ed.) (1989) *Hopkins in Lancashire: Selected Writings of Gerard Manley Hopkins*. Wigan: North West Catholic History Society

McDermott, J., (ed.) (1994) *Hopkins' Lancashire Sesquicentennial Essays*. Wigan: North West Catholic History Society

Paxton A. and Higgins, L. (2014) 'A Memoir of "Uncle Gerard" by Beatrice Handley-Derry'. *The Hopkins Quarterly*. Vol. XLI No.s 3-4, pp 57-68

Ryan, N. (1948) *St. Francis Xavier's Church, Liverpool Centenary 1848-1948*. Liverpool: Kilburns

Thornton, R.K.R. and Phillips, C. (2013) *The Collected Works of Gerard Manley Hopkins: Volumes I and II: Correspondence*. Oxford: O.U.P.

Offshoots

The two poems quoted in full in this book have inspired other responses, which may be of interest to readers.

Felix Randal

In the play *Felix Randal*, Jimmy McGovern (b.1949) imagines the events which might have led Hopkins to compose the poem about the Liverpool farrier.
It was broadcast as *The Afternoon Play* on BBC Radio 4 in October 1985.

The poem has been set to music a number of times, including by:

- Gary Bachland (b. 1947).

- David Stanhope (b.1952).

- Sean O'Leary (b.1953).

Spring and Fall

The title of *Margaret*, Kenneth Lonergan's 2011 film, is a reference to 'Spring and Fall'. The poem is read out to a class about half way through the film

Musical settings have been completed by:

- Vivian Fine (1913-2000).

- Stephen Wilkinson (b.1919).

- Peter Westergaard (b. 1931).
- Alexandra Pierce (b. 1934).
- Stephen R. Geber (b. 1948).
- Paul Kelly (b.1955), whose 2012 album was called *Spring and Fall*.
- John Peterson (b. 1957).
- Natalie Merchant (b. 1963).
- Aaron Alon.

A Hopkins Walk

The following walk allows you to wander past many of the places in and around Lydiate that Hopkins might have known.

However, it's been designed as a pleasant wander, taking in plenty of attractive scenery, and interesting places along the way.

It will take about three hours, without stops, and there is a cafe and several pubs along the route.

If you prefer driving to travelling by train, there is parking at and near both Maghull and Town Green Station, and, of course, the walk can be adapted to suit your preference.

For a shorter version of the walk, concentrating on the significant places mentioned in this book, PLEASE BEGIN HERE ***.
You'll need a car for this one!

Begin at **Maghull Station** (5 minutes)

Turn **RIGHT** as you leave the station, past the Great Mogul pub, and turn onto Station Road.

On the wall of a large house set back on your left, you'll see the blue plaque which commemorates Frank Hornby, the toy manufacturer.

Turn second **LEFT,** walking to the end of Rutherford Drive.

As you climb over the canal bridge, look **RIGHT** - which is the direction you'll be walking in. You double back on yourself at the foot of the bridge, then turning **LEFT** and walking along the canal, away from the railway.

The **Canal Path** (35-40 minutes)

This peaceful towpath runs past a number of swing (as well as road) bridges. You'll pass under the A59, and past parks, canal-side homes and the back of Maghull town centre (on your right).

After a while, countryside will appear on your left, and the Running Horses pub. Look out for the narrow boat turning point on your right, then leave the path at bridge number 17, turning **LEFT** down Pilling Lane.

49

Towards the **Old Railway** (10-15 minutes)

*** *[BEGIN THE SHORTER WALK HERE,*
parking on the west or rural side of the Pilling Lane bridge] ***

Continue down Pilling Lane for a couple of hundred metres.

As the lane bends sharply to your right, look for the footpath sign on the bend's **LEFT** hand corner, marked "Public Footpath Altcar Lane".

The path follows the **LEFT** hand side of a field for about 400 metres.

When you reach Altcar Lane, turn **LEFT** and immediately **RIGHT** down Cabin Lane. This can be muddy, but walkers have 'created' a parallel path in the field on your **RIGHT**.

After a couple of hundred metres, turn **RIGHT** onto the old Southport and South Cheshire Lines Extension railway path.

The Railway Path (10 minutes)

After about five hundred metres, you'll reach the site of Lydiate's old station. No part of the building remains, but there is a small sign. Continue along the railway path for another five hundred metres or so.

Turn **RIGHT** at the wood on your right.

Towards Lydiate Hall (15 minutes)

Follow this path for 200 metres to Acres Lane. Turn **LEFT** on to the lane and (very soon) turn **RIGHT** onto the footpath leading uphill, marked "Lyd No. 20 Southport 3/4".

When a wood appears on your **LEFT**, follow the path anti-clockwise around its edge. In winter/ early spring, you'll get a first view of the ruins of Lydiate Hall, through the trees.

The path takes you up onto Southport Road (the A5147).

50

Old Lydiate (30-40 minutes)

Turn **RIGHT** and walk down to St. Catherine's Chapel ruins and the Scotch Piper. Then, retrace your steps, past the head of the footpath and turn **LEFT** off Southport Road and down the track to the Hayloft, farm shop and Lydiate Hall.
There is a short walk through the wood beyond the Hall, where the bulbs are very attractive in spring.
Return down the track and cross the main road onto Hall Lane. Our Lady's Church is on your right - the Lightbound marbled grave is to the left of its path.

Leaving the churchyard, continue down Hall Lane for about 300 metres and turn **RIGHT** onto the footpath marked "Public Footpath Lollies Bridge 1/2)".
Follow the winding footpath over a rise, across a gallop (twice) and past several paddocks, until you walk over the bridge and the Leeds and Liverpool Canal.
Turn **RIGHT** and follow the path above the canal for about 100 metres. At the footpath sign, turn **LEFT** up the slope and onto Sandy Lane. Follow the Lane for about 400 metres and turn **LEFT** onto the footpath opposite Silver Birch Way.
Follow the footpath for about 100 metres, turning **RIGHT** at the arrow and **RIGHT** again towards a group of farm buildings. The footpath passes round to their **RIGHT**, rejoining Moss Lane.

Around and beyond Rose Hill House (30-40 minutes for the main walk)

Turn **LEFT** and continue for about 400 metres along the footpath on the left hand side of Moss Lane.
Turn **LEFT** on to the footpath marked "Pygons Hill Lane". Rose Hill House is on your left, where the footpath meets Pygons Hill Lane.

*** *[TO CONTINUE THE SHORTER WALK*
SEE THE BOTTOM OF P. 50] ***

To continue with the main walk, turn LEFT past the house, and Rose Hill Farm, and continue down the lane for about 500 metres, turning **RIGHT**

51

into Sudell Lane. Cross into Lancashire over Sudell Brook, and after about 500 metres, turn **LEFT** into Back Lane, following it to its end at Hollin House Green Farm.

Take the **RIGHT** hand footpath in front of the farm, following the farm buildings, now on your **LEFT**, and bear **RIGHT** at a hedge, taking you towards more farm buildings. Turn **LEFT** and follow the footpath on the **LEFT** of a hedge towards the A59.

Cross the dual carriageway with care and then walk up its **RIGHT** hand side for about 300 metres and take the footpath on your **RIGHT** across a small field, bearing **LEFT** and then to the **RIGHT** of an old barn. Walk down the drive of a house, and you emerge at Church Lane.

Turn **RIGHT** and walk past The Stanley Arms and St. Michael's Church.

Turn **LEFT** down Ron Gordon Way - the footpath opposite St. Michael's lychgate - following it through a wood and bearing **RIGHT** after about 400 metres.

Town Green (10 minutes)
Cross the footbridge in the corner and then turn **LEFT** onto Town Green's playing fields. Walk under the trees, turning **RIGHT** on to Winifred Lane and then **LEFT** on to Town Green Lane. Town Green Station is on your right.

***THE SECOND HALF OF THE SHORTER WALK
(from Rose Hill onwards. Allow 30 minutes)***

Continue past Rose Hill House and along Pygons Hill Lane for about 800 metres until you reach the road/ canal bridge.

*Before the bridge, turn **LEFT** on to the canal track and follow this as it becomes a path for about 600 metres, until you reach the next bridge over the canal.*

*Cross the canal and immediately take the steps to your **LEFT**, then turning **RIGHT** onto the towpath. Follow this for about one kilometre, until you arrive back at Pilling Lane.*